Community Development Financial Institutions Response to Superstorm Sandy

Impact Assessment

On November 14, 2012, CDFI Fund Director Donna J. Gambrell sent a letter to Community Development Financial Institutions to assess the impact of Superstorm Sandy. This report provides the results collected by the CDFI Fund.

Contents

Among the first projects that the Low Income Investment Fund (LIIF) supported through its $1 million commitment to communities affected by Superstorm Sandy was St. John's Bread & Life, an emergency food provider in New York City.

"Although there may be many other sources of financing from the government as well as the banking community, we know that our CDFI capital is generally more flexible and can play a part in many deals even where mainstream financing is available from other sources."

David C. Raynor, Executive Director, Leviticus 25:23 Alternative Fund, Inc.

Introduction

Community Development Financial Institutions—or CDFIs—emerged in response to a lack of access to responsible and affordable credit and capital in minority and economically distressed communities. Today, with the help of the Community Development Financial Institutions Fund (CDFI Fund), part of the U.S. Department of the Treasury, what started as a grassroots movement has grown into a thriving sector of the financial services industry that is meeting the needs of communities across the nation.

In October 2012, one of the largest storms to ever hit the East Coast, Superstorm Sandy, created devastation on an epic scale. I knew that CDFIs would play a vital role in recovery efforts in the areas impacted by the storm. CDFIs, day in and day out, are on the front lines providing vital financing and services to underserved communities across our country.

In order to assess the impact of Superstorm Sandy on CDFIs and the people and communities they serve, I sent a brief survey to the CDFI Fund's certified CDFIs and Community Development Entities (CDEs). As the CDFI Fund has come to expect from CDFIs, they came through for their clients in a time of great hardship. The following survey responses by CDFIs exemplify the dedication and mission of these vital organizations to helping people and communities most in need.

CDFIs have and will continue to play an extremely important role in supporting the recovery in those communities on the East Coast that are in dire need at this time. The CDFI Fund stands ready to provide the help needed for the marathon of rebuilding that is yet to come.

Donna J. Gambrell
CDFI Fund Director

Executive Summary

On November 14, 2012, the CDFI Fund sent a letter to CDFIs to assess the impact of Superstorm Sandy on CDFIs and their clients. In conducting this brief, voluntary assessment, the CDFI Fund sought to identify the needs of CDFIs and areas in which the CDFI Fund could be most helpful.

The CDFI Fund recognized that obtaining responses from CDFIs during the height of this emergency would be challenging. The CDFI Fund did not expect a large response because many of the CDFIs in the affected region were still battling the effects of the storm, but wanted to begin assessing the future needs of CDFIs as soon as possible. The CDFI Fund is grateful for the responses received from 13 CDFIs in the region. The following are key findings from the respondents.

- Of the CDFIs that responded, 10 had some damage to their offices, i.e., no electricity, heat, phone, Internet, etc. One respondent, Enterprise Community Partners, sustained serious damage and flooding in its New York office. It is interesting to note that of the 10 CDFIs that experienced physical damage, six out of the 10 remained operational.

- Of the CDFIs that sustained damage, all have reopened for business (two never closed). Three respondents reopened on October 31; one reopened on November 2; five reopened on November 5; one on November 17; and Enterprise Community Partners, which withstood the most severe damage, reopened on November 29.

- Not a single respondent stated that the CDFI itself needed any help; however, two respondents did request funding to help their clients. Business Outreach Center Capital suggested that the CDFI Fund provide low- to no-interest capital so that CDFIs could provide recovery loans and/or have sufficient loan loss reserves to support the riskier disaster recovery loans.[1]

- Of the 10 CDFIs that endured damage, all 10 also had clients who were impacted by Superstorm Sandy.

- The CDFI Fund asked if any of the CDFIs are currently involved in or providing direct recovery assistance services. Of the nine respondents, two stated that they are not presently providing direct recovery assistance services (as of November 14, 2012), but are developing disaster recovery loan funds to assist small businesses affected by Superstorm Sandy. Since the time of the survey, Accion has established a small business loan fund. Other respondents reported the following direct recovery efforts:

  o **Business Outreach Center Capital** has launched a disaster recovery loan program for any small business that was physically and/or financially impacted by the storm throughout the five boroughs of New York City.

  o **Community Development Corporation of Long Island** is working on a coordinated effort with local community leaders to attend community meetings and go door-to-door in the hardest hit communities to develop a housing needs assessment.

---

[1] The CDFI Fund is taking all suggestions under advisement. It should be noted that the CDFI Fund can provide grants to CDFIs under the CDFI Program for uses such as loan loss reserves. Other suggestions found in this document fall outside the authority of the CDFI Fund and would need Congressional action.

- o **Empire State Development Corporation** (in partnership with the Governor's office) launched a number of assistance programs to address the needs and concerns of the businesses in the areas affected by Superstorm Sandy.

- o **Enterprise Community Partners** has launched the Partner Support and Rebuilding Fund (Fund) to provide financial assistance to help its affordable housing partners with immediate recovery and rebuilding efforts.

- o The **Low Income Investment Fund** has committed $1 million to ensure that those hardest hit by the storm have access to food and much needed services.

- o **Primary Care Development Corporation** and the Community Health Care Association of New York City (CHCANYS) co-direct the Primary Care Emergency Preparedness Network (PCEPN), a New York City Department of Health and Mental Hygiene initiative to provide primary care representation at the New York City Emergency Operations Center (EOC). Before, during, and after the storm, PCEPN enabled a core group of approximately 27 primary care networks representing over 90 primary care locations throughout New York City to stay updated about storm situations, resources, and recovery efforts.

- o **Seedco Financial Services** is developing the initial phase of a Small Business Recovery Initiative that will be geared to address a targeted set of disaster recovery related needs for small businesses that suffered from storm-related impact.

Snap food truck (Elizabeth Courtney)
Brooklyn, New York
CDFI: Business Outreach Center Capital

The Red Hook section of Brooklyn was hit particularly hard with most businesses sustaining both physical damage and financial loss. Snap Food Truck, a client of BOC Capital, was able to move its vehicle out of the flood zone, but the industrial kitchen space used to store and prepare food was flooded, soiling inventory and equipment and remained without power and hot water for weeks. There was a financial cost as the food truck was without much of its inventory and was unable to relocate to more unaffected areas due to fuel shortages. BOC Capital is working with this client by applying a 30-day loan deferment and periods of interest-only payments to help free up cash for recovery. Additionally, BOC Capital is working with and on behalf of the business to identify potential recovery loans, grants and financial strategies to help support losses. Ongoing needs include additional low-interest capital (or grants) to help replace equipment and to locate a new kitchen space to support business operations and growth.

About the CDFI Fund

In 1994, the Community Development Financial Institutions Fund (CDFI Fund) was created for the purpose of promoting economic and community development through investment in and assistance to Community Development Financial Institutions (CDFIs). The CDFI Fund supports the mission-driven financial institutions working on a local level that know their communities best. Financial institutions that become certified by the CDFI Fund are eligible to apply for the comprehensive services it offers— including monetary support and training to build organization capacity. The CDFI Fund's model is competitive and each of its programs provides CDFIs with the flexibility to determine the best use of limited federal resources in their communities. The CDFI Fund makes an impact through a wide range of innovative programs.

- CDFI Program: Provides Financial Assistance and Technical Assistance awards to certified and emerging CDFIs to sustain and expand their services and to build their technical capacity.

- Native Initiatives: Includes the Native American CDFI Assistance Program, which provides Financial Assistance and Technical Assistance awards to CDFIs serving Native communities to sustain and expand their services and to build their technical capacity; and training opportunities for Native CDFIs available as part of the CDFI Fund's Capacity Building Initiative.

- Bank Enterprise Award Program: Provides monetary awards to Federal Deposit Insurance Corporation insured banks for increasing their investments in low-income communities and/or in CDFIs.

- New Markets Tax Credit Program: Provides tax allocation authority to certified Community Development Entities (CDEs), enabling investors to claim tax credits against their federal income taxes. The CDEs, in turn, use the capital raised to make investments in low-income communities.

- Capacity Building Initiative: Provides organizations certified as CDFIs or trying to become CDFIs with access to free seminars, market research and analysis, tools, and one-on-one training to help them develop, diversify, and grow.

- CDFI Bond Guarantee Program: Guarantees the full amount of notes or bonds issued to support CDFIs that make investments for eligible community or economic development purposes. These bonds or notes support CDFI lending and investment by providing a source of long-term, patient capital.[2]

---

[2] The CDFI Bond Guarantee Program is currently awaiting Congressional approval of required appropriations language that provides the authority to issue bonds.

"Over the course of the past 10 years, Seedco Financial Services has operated small business disaster recovery programs following both natural and manmade disasters in New York City and Louisiana. With more than a decade of expertise in helping small businesses and communities with economic relief and disaster recovery services, Seedco Financial Services has developed institutional capacity to mobilize and deploy critical support, including providing access to grant and loan capital, overseeing the development and delivery of direct technical assistance services, and promoting and aligning support for other ongoing small business recovery efforts."

Edwin Hong, COO, Seedco Financial Services, Inc.

Photos of the East River flooding one of Seedco Financial Services' small business clients, a restaurant named Suteshi, and the resulting damage.

What is a CDFI?

CDFIs are specialized, community-based financial institutions that serve low-income people and organizations in economically distressed communities, often working in market niches that may be underserved by traditional financial institutions. Only financial institutions certified by the CDFI Fund can receive Financial Assistance awards through the CDFI Program and the NACA Program. Technical Assistance awards are available through both programs to certified CDFIs and entities that propose to become certified CDFIs.

CDFIs provide a unique and wide range of financial products and services. While the types of products made available are generally similar to those provided by mainstream financial institutions (such as mortgage financing for low-income and first-time homebuyers, small business lending, and lending for community facilities), CDFIs often lend to and make equity investments in markets that may not be served by mainstream financial institutions. In addition, CDFIs may offer rates and terms that are more flexible to low-income borrowers. CDFIs also provide services that help ensure that credit is used effectively, such as technical assistance to small businesses and home buying and credit counseling to consumers. CDFIs include depository institutions, such as community development banks and credit unions, and non-depository institutions, such as loan funds and venture capital funds.

What is a CDE?

Through the New Markets Tax Credit Program, the CDFI Fund allocates tax credit authority to Community Development Entities (CDEs) through a competitive application process. CDEs are financial intermediaries through which investment capital flows from an investor to a qualified business located in a low-income community. CDEs use their authority to offer tax credits to investors in exchange for equity in the CDE. With these capital investments, CDEs can make loans and investments to businesses operating in distressed areas that have better rates and terms and more flexible features than the market.

To become certified as a CDE, an organization must submit a CDE Certification Application to the CDFI Fund for review. The application must demonstrate that the applicant meets each of the following requirements to become certified:

- Be a legal entity at the time of application;
- Have a primary mission of serving LICs; and
- Maintain accountability to the residents of its targeted LICs.

Photo of a damaged small business client of Community Development Corporation of Long Island. The small business is located in Bay Shore, New York.

Vineland Crossing Grocery & Retail Center
Vineland, New Jersey
CDE: CCG Community Partners

CCG Community Partners, a Treasury-certified CDE, assembled the key New Markets Tax Credit equity financing for the $24.6 million development of the Vineland Crossing Grocery & Retail Center in Vineland, New Jersey. Vineland Crossing consists of a ShopRite grocery store, a non-profit federally-qualified health clinic and pharmacy, and three additional retail units. It is in a Federally-designated Medically Underserved Area and Food Deserts Census Tract.

Vineland Crossing is estimated to create 200 new construction jobs while retaining approximately 135 existing full- and part-time jobs and creating an additional 75 new full- and part-time jobs in a census tract with a 35.8 percent poverty rate, 32.7 percent median family income, and 26.2 percent unemployment rate. Vineland Crossing will provide downtown Vineland and the surrounding community with a full-service supermarket offering increased varieties of healthy food choices at competitive pricing while participating in Special Supplemental Nutrition Programs such as electronic food stamps and WIC (Women, Infants, and Children) assistance programs for qualifying low-income individuals.

In addition, the retail shopping center will feature a Federally Qualified Health Clinic serving 5,000 patients a year, as well as a pharmacy participating in the 340B Drug Pricing Program. It is anticipated that the Vineland Crossing project will catalyze further retail development in the Landis Avenue Corridor, which will in turn lead to additional economic development in downtown Vineland.

In the wake of Superstorm Sandy, Vineland Crossing experienced site flooding and power loss. Construction materials, such as steel, were delayed by the breakdown of regional infrastructure, and the project's construction schedule is suffering additional delays and material cost increases. The Sponsor is thus incurring additional costs, and many of its sister stores and warehouse locations were significantly impacted. The Sponsor, part of a larger supermarket conglomerate, participated in Sandy Relief Efforts by providing food and funds with the Wakefern Food Corp, which donated $1 million in both funds and in-kind goods focusing on regional food banks. In the hours following the storm, individual stores began addressing the needs of their communities by providing food, water, and ice to local charities and governmental agencies.

"As a leading microfinance organization, Accion has focused its response on the most credit challenged businesses impacted by Superstorm Sandy. Accion's fast, simple, and flexible grant and loan solution is part of the New York CDFI's effort to lead the recovery from the bottom up."

Paul Quintero, CEO, Accion East

Findings: Impact Assessment

CDFIs have a proven record of successfully mobilizing private sector resources to achieve positive community development impact, especially in times of greatest need. CDFIs are on the front lines providing vital financing and services to underserved communities across our country before, during, and after a crisis. CDFIs have and will play an extremely important role in supporting the recovery in those communities on the East Coast that are in dire need from the devastation caused by Superstorm Sandy.

On November 14, 2012, CDFI Fund Director Donna J. Gambrell sent a letter to CDFIs to assess the impact of Superstorm Sandy on CDFIs and their clients.[3] In conducting this brief, voluntary survey, the CDFI Fund sought to identify the needs of CDFIs and areas in which the CDFI Fund could be most helpful.

The CDFI Fund received 13 responses to its inquiry. The respondents are:

- Accion USA & Accion East
- Business Outreach Center Capital (BOC)
- CCG Community Partners
- Community Development Corporation of Long Island (CDC of Long Island)
- Enterprise Community Partners
- Empire State Development Corporation
- Leviticus 25:23 Alternative Fund, Inc.
- Low Income Investment Fund (LIIF)
- Nonprofit Financing Fund (NFF)
- New Jersey Community Capital
- Primary Care Development Corporation (PCDC)
- Seedco Financial Services (SFS)
- The Disability Opportunity Fund (DOF)

---

[3] In the region most impacted by Superstorm Sandy, there are 114 U.S. Treasury certified CDFIs and 1,402 CDEs, including subsidiaries. Specifically, there are 15 certified CDFIs and 40 CDEs (including subsidiaries) in Connecticut that have received a total of almost $94 million in CDFI Fund awards and New Markets Tax Credits (NMTCs). In New Jersey, there are 17 certified CDFIs and 108 CDEs (including subsidiaries) that have received over $530 million in CDFI Fund awards and tax credits. Finally, there are 82 CDFIs in New York and 553 CDEs (including subsidiaries) that have received more than $4.5 billion in CDFI Fund awards and NMTCs.

The following provides the questions asked by the CDFI Fund and a summary of the responses received.

Was your CDFI impacted by Superstorm Sandy? If so, how?

Responses: 12

Of the CDFIs that responded, 10 had some damage to their offices, i.e., no electricity, heat, phone, Internet, etc. One respondent, Enterprise Community Partners, sustained serious damage and flooding in its New York office. Additionally, many of the staff of these CDFIs had the same problems at home: power outages, gas shortages, dangerous transportation conditions, and/or flooding.

It is interesting to note that of the 10 CDFIs that experienced physical damage, six out of the 10 remained operational. Due to resource diversification and sheer determination, staff kept working. Those that had power worked from home and those that didn't found a location with power and some type of phone/internet access to stay in touch with clients.

Just one example is Primary Care Development Corporation. PCDC has an emergency preparedness plan, which it activated. This included preparing staff to work at home for an indefinite period, communicating via a Google groups listserv that connected to PCDC staff personal emails; holding daily staff conference calls; and notifying key contacts about PCDC's situation and alternate communications. While business was interrupted, many of PCDC's staff were able to conduct business remotely, including completing payroll a day after the storm hit.

One CDFI did have costs to rescue its server and computer systems, but was eventually able to "connect" through staff's mobile devices. This CDFI is considering moving its server to a more secure location connected to a natural-gas generator to keep its lines of communication open in the future.

One CDE, CCG Community Partners, was directly in the path of Superstorm Sandy, yet at all times its data and communications were secure because diversification is part of the organization's overall strategic planning. CCG Community Partners' mission is to invest in communities that have been impacted by disasters (whether natural, man-made, or economic) with a priority focus on job creation and core services such as food, medicine, shelter, and education in sustainable platforms for transformative outcomes. "This concept has been our consistent message since our very first investment in New Orleans, made after Hurricane Katrina devastated New Orleans and the Gulf Opportunity Zone. We have followed with investments in areas hit hardest by subsequent hurricanes, flooding, tornados, and the BP Oil Disaster."

"Thanks to funds from the CDFI Fund's Financial Assistance program and specifically the Healthy Food Financing Initiative, the Low Income Investment Fund is already providing subsidized loans and grants to organizations responding to and affected by the hurricane. LIIF has committed $1 million for immediate relief efforts for victims of Sandy and expects to invest more as the longer-term needs of communities become clear during the recovery and rebuilding of the region. LIIF is grateful to the CDFI Fund for its support and for encouraging CDFIs to collectively use their networks and resources to help those in need in the wake of this disaster."

    Judith Kende, Senior Vice President, Eastern and Central Regions, Low Income Investment Fund

Have you reopened for business, and if so when?
Responses: 12

Of the CDFIs that sustained damage, all have reopened for business (two never closed). Three respondents reopened on October 31, 2012; one reopened on November 2; five reopened on November 5, 2012; one on November 17, 2012; and Enterprise Community Partners, which withstood the most severe damage, reopened on November 29, 2012.

What are your needs moving forward?
Responses: 4

Not a single respondent stated that the CDFI itself needed any help; however, two respondents did request funding to help their clients. Business Outreach Center Capital suggested that the CDFI Fund provide low- to no-interest capital so that CDFIs could provide recovery loans and/or have sufficient loan loss reserves to support the riskier disaster recovery loans.[4]

CCG Community Partners stated that over 97 percent of its prior NMTC allocations are already invested in projects that meet the highest indicia of distress. Currently, they have no additional NMTCs to focus on the areas destroyed by Superstorm Sandy. CCG Community Partners suggested that if the CDFI Fund currently has any returned NMTC allocations from prior awardees that it reallocate the NMTCs for redeployment into the hardest hit communities.[5]

Amadou Ba: Taxi Driver
Brooklyn, New York
CDFI: Business Outreach Center Capital

Amadou Ba is a livery service provider located in Brooklyn, New York, who was affected by the storm's impact on the availability of fuel. Mr. Ba as well as hundreds of car service providers sustained considerable financial loss because without fuel they were unable to operate. As power began to return to storm affected areas, Mr. Ba often had to drive out of state to Connecticut and Pennsylvania to find fuel to support his business and personal expenses. BOC Capital has provided a 30-day deferment on Mr. Ba's outstanding loan balance as well as interest-only payments for three months to help support positive cash flow.

[4] Ibid at 1, page 3.
[5] Congressional approval is needed to implement this suggestion.

Are you currently involved in or providing any direct recovery assistance services?

Responses: 9

Of the nine respondents, two stated that they are not presently providing direct recovery assistance services (as of November 14, 2012), but are developing disaster recovery loan funds to assist small businesses affected by Superstorm Sandy. Since the time of the survey, Accion has established a small business loan fund (see page 19 for more details).

Other respondents reported the following direct recovery efforts:

Business Outreach Center Capital has launched a disaster recovery loan program for any small business that was physically and/or financially impacted by the storm throughout the five boroughs of New York City. The CDFI is working with and supporting New York City and New York State recovery efforts for small business by providing referrals, links, and resources to disaster recovery programs and initiatives, as well as facilitating intake and packaging when necessary.

Community Development Corporation of Long Island is working on a coordinated effort with local community leaders to attend community meetings and go door-to-door in the hardest hit communities to develop a housing needs assessment. CDC of Long Island has also reached out to their small business clients, assessing damage and providing them with information and counseling on all available resources. Most recently, CDC of Long Island was awarded a contract to administer the FEMA STEP program on behalf of Suffolk County. STEP provides temporary repairs to allow individuals to return to their homes while long-term repairs are made.

Empire State Development Corporation (in partnership with the Governor's office) launched a number of assistance programs to address the needs and concerns of the businesses in the areas affected by Superstorm Sandy. These include the institution of a $10-million Small Business Revolving Loan Fund.

Enterprise Community Partners has launched the Partner Support and Rebuilding Fund (Fund) to provide financial assistance to help its affordable housing partners with immediate recovery and rebuilding efforts. The Fund consists of two components: emergency grants to be used to address any immediate needs resulting from the storm, including purchasing of supplies, equipment, deposits, and fees needed to hire contractors, and/or other resources to support displaced families; and low-cost working capital for affordable housing development partners to use to speed rebuilding, including bridging the gap to other resources (including public resources) and insurance coverage. (See page 20 for additional information.)

The **Low Income Investment Fund** has committed $1 million to ensure that those hardest hit by the storm have access to food and much needed services. LIIF's New York staff has reached out to its local network to understand the needs in the communities that it serves. As a result, LIIF is providing deeply subsidized loans and grants to grocery stores and social service non-profit clients that operate in areas of high need, such as the Rockaways, Coney Island, and Staten Island. These organizations can use the funds for inventory, facilities repair, and working capital so they can re-establish themselves in their local communities. (See page 21 for additional information.)

Primary Care Development Corporation, prior to Superstorm Sandy, had already developed several disaster preparedness programs. These include the *Emergency Preparedness for Primary Health Care in Underserved Communities,* a technical assistance program that includes robust emergency preparedness services. Through this program, PCDC has provided emergency management and business continuity services to more than 200 primary care centers, primary care associations, and long-term care facilities across the United States, including nearly 80 serving more than 500,000 patients in low-income New York City communities. PCDC's services include emergency planning, staff training, drills and exercises, and community/regional planning.

In addition, PCDC and the Community Health Care Association of New York City (CHCANYS) co-direct the Primary Care Emergency Preparedness Network (PCEPN), a New York City Department of Health and Mental Hygiene initiative to provide primary care representation at the New York City Emergency Operations Center (EOC). The EOC is activated during emergencies for senior officials from City, State, and Federal agencies, as well as other entities to coordinate response efforts, centralize decision making, disseminate information, and allocate resources. Before, during, and after the storm, PCEPN enabled a core group of approximately 27 primary care networks representing over 90 primary care locations throughout New York City to stay updated about storm situations, resources, and recovery efforts. PCEPN was able to successfully support primary care centers by linking them with non-government organizations to receive donations of medications and supplies, and is in communication with members regarding FEMA applications and other relief efforts. PCEPN staff also played a role in New York City Healthcare Facility Evacuation Center (HEC) by supporting the evacuation of healthcare facilities that faced the highest risk of flooding.

Anne Buckley-Reen: Pediatric Occupational Therapist
Belle Harbor, New York (Rockaways)
CDFI: Business Outreach Center Capital

Anne Buckley-Reen is a pediatric occupational therapist and president of For Kids Pediatric OT located in Belle Harbor, NY (The Rockaways) that provides Occupational Therapy and Yoga Therapy for students with developmental challenges. The Rockaways sustained substantial direct damage from the storm and Anne's home and business were flooded beyond the 1st floor with power outages lasting for weeks. Hurricane Sandy not only damaged and stranded Anne in her home but also destroyed much of her business equipment and supplies as well as loss of business revenue. Anne came to BOC Capital to apply for a disaster recovery loan and after receiving some direct Technical Assistance regarding disaster recovery strategies and resources, Anne was approved for a $10,000 recovery loan to help re-create inventory used for educational purposes to get her business back on track. Anne, like many businesses in the area, will need ongoing assistance both in capital and support resources to rebuild her business and help support her community.

CDFI Response to Superstorm Sandy

East End Disability Associates, Inc.
Long Island, New York
CDFI: The Disability Opportunity Fund

East End Disability Associates, Inc. (EEDA) is a nonprofit organization that provides supports and services for people with developmental disabilities on Long Island. Its various programs include "respite services" for children with varying disabilities. During Superstorm Sandy, the home being rented by EEDA to provide respite services was inadequate to handle the loss of power and was forced to close for a number of weeks. EEDA's management approached the Disability Opportunity Fund (DOF), a certified CDFI, with an idea to purchase their own home that they could prepare for continual services in the event of other events, weather-related or otherwise. They have already received donations for a down-payment on the house; DOF will finance the acquisition and minor renovations for this home (approximately $500,000).

Seedco Financial Services is developing the initial phase of a Small Business Recovery Initiative that will be geared to address a targeted set of disaster recovery related needs for small businesses that suffered from storm-related impact. SFS's immediate aim is to target a highly-impacted location in New York City and focus on addressing the needs of one or more of the community's critical small business sectors. SFS is currently engaged in a targeted fundraising effort from primarily private sector funding sources in order to support the launch of the initial phase of this initiative. SFS hopes to include small business disaster recovery loans; disaster-related technical assistance; loan application filing assistance; insurance claims filing assistance; and lease re-negotiation services.

Have any of your clients been impacted?
Responses: 10

Of the 10 CDFIs that endured damage, all 10 also had clients who were impacted by Superstorm Sandy. Below are just a few examples of the storm's effect on CDFI clients.

Business Outreach Center Capital reached out to all loan clients (current and past) to assess impact and to see what (if any) support was needed. Business Outreach Center Capital has provided a 30-day, interest-only payment period to any current loan client that has been negatively impacted by the storm, and continues to work with and assess the capital needs of those most harshly affected. Business Outreach Center Capital has many clients located throughout New York City, with particular emphasis on Lower Manhattan and Brooklyn, which have been negatively impacted by the storm, either through direct physical damage and/or as a result of power outage and fuel shortages.

One of the Community Development Corporation of Long Island's small business loan clients was a restaurant near the water that was almost completely destroyed.

"New York City along with other private partnerships has announced a matching grant program to provide up to $10,000 in grant monies to match loans approved through their emergency loan program. Requirements for the loan program and subsequent grant include a minimum average credit score of all business owners 20 percent or more of 650 and that a business has filed its 2011 tax returns. Many of the businesses that BOC Capital Corp works with (and operate within BOC's targeted areas) fall outside of these minimum criteria, and as such would not qualify for the loan or the matching grant. It is BOC Capital's goal to support the capital needs incurred by our target businesses as result of this disaster and have recommended to expand the matching grant program to include approved disaster loans through BOC Capital and other local CDFIs."

Nancy Carin, Executive Director, BOC Capital Corp.

One of Enterprise Community Partner's projects, Surf Garden Coney Island, had to be evacuated and experienced flooding, water and mud on the ground floor, which also damaged the heating and elevator systems. Enterprise Community Partners has several additional properties that experienced flooded basements in lower Manhattan and Brooklyn that have damaged heating and/or water systems. Additionally, a number of properties have reported some damage to exterior walls, the roof, and associated water damage. In New Jersey, Enterprise Community Partners has several properties that did not have damage, but they did have extended periods without power and were able to rely on generators.

Unfortunately, many of the communities that the Low Income Investment Fund invests in were seriously affected by Superstorm Sandy and continue to grapple with the storm's lingering effects. Among LIIF's clients, grocery store owners and operators were among the worst hit. These small businesses are often run by individuals or families, who operate on already thin margins. With damage to their facilities, ongoing power outages and supply chain disruption, these entrepreneurs are in a particularly precarious position. In addition, LIIF specifically invests in grocery stores operating in food deserts, so the closure of these stores has a ripple effect for communities that already lack access to food.

The Nonprofit Finance Fund had one former borrower that sustained several millions of dollars of damage to its community center and is unable to provide services in that space. The Nonprofit Finance Fund is providing a $300,000 low-interest bridge loan so it can begin recovery and rebuilding.

Many of New Jersey Community Capital's clients were impacted because they do all of their work in the coastal areas of New Jersey, which were some of the hardest hit areas from the storm. Immediate needs included temporary housing for those displaced; short-term funding for businesses that sustained some damage but were able to open and operate relatively quickly; and assistance to put some "normalcy" back into people's lives.

Most of the Primary Care Development Corporation's clients that were in the path of Superstorm Sandy were closed temporarily and suffered revenue losses. Only one of PCDC's borrowers, the Addabbo Family Health Center, incurred significant damage to its facilities and operations. Two-thirds of Addabbo's operations are near New York City's waterfront, including the Rockaway Peninsula and Red Hook, Brooklyn. Management estimates that the temporary closure of these locations will result in operating losses of approximately $1 million (about 3 percent of annual revenues).

Displaced Family
Long Beach, New York
CDFI: The Disability Opportunity Fund

Todd and Kim G. have four children, two of whom have been diagnosed with Autism Spectrum Disorder, live in a home located in Long Beach, New York. They were forced to evacuate the home during Superstorm Sandy and upon returning to the home the day after the storm, found that the first floor was gone since their home was hit by both the bay and the ocean.

They were moved to a hotel in Garden City funded by FEMA. In addition to being displaced, the added stress of moving two young children with Autism Spectrum Disorder into an unfamiliar setting has proven very difficult. In addition, their new "neighbors" in the hotel have been less than understanding of their children's mannerisms. To top it off, FEMA announced that they would stop payments for the hotel come mid-January.

A call to Autism Speaks directed this family to the Disability Opportunity Fund (DOF), which located a house that they can rent until the Long Beach home is repaired. The rental home will need some minor renovations/adjustments to suit this family. DOF has committed funds (approximately $75,000) to help this family get into transitional housing.

PCDC is seeing two trends emerging among those clients directly impacted: first, they were closed for a minimum of two and as many as 10 days, due primarily to loss of power. These clients estimate the associated loss of revenues to range from $200,000 up to $2 million (as much as 4 percent of annual revenues). The second and more significant trend was lower visit volumes (sometimes materially lower) even for those clients that reopened quickly and were fully staffed. This appears to be the result of health center clientele attending to more immediate post-storm matters. The financial impact of this trend is difficult to quantify as it is evolving in terms of patient visits and staffing, but it potentially represents the longest-term risk to PCDC's clients.

Although these healthcare facilities should be able to recoup some losses from business interruption insurance, which covers closures, a drop in business due to the subsequent effects of a storm is not covered. As such, in an industry with thin margins, this threatens to turn positive operations to negative. It should be noted that as part of PCDC's loan covenants, borrowers are required to carry business interruption insurance and, if they are in a flood zone, flood insurance.

One of Seedco Financial Services clients suffered from extensive physical damage due to flooding in downtown Manhattan. The client operates a street-level, full-service restaurant in South Street Seaport district. Tidal surge from the East River flowed throughout the restaurant location; as a result, the business owner incurred a total loss of equipment and inventory and must engage in gut renovation of the leased space. Seedco Financial Services estimates that business operations will be closed for a three- to four-month period. Another client operates a street-level, full service restaurant and chocolate production business in the Financial District of lower Manhattan. This location suffered from significant damage due to flooding from the East River and Hudson River Bay and is now closed until further notice as the business owners evaluate their resources and options. In addition, Seedco Financial Services has a number of clients with business operations in impacted areas of Staten Island, Queens, Brooklyn, and Manhattan.

One group that was not impacted by Superstorm Sandy was due to a loan provided for a small group home in Westchester, New York by the Disability Opportunity Fund. The client used the loan to purchase a generator for "future" emergencies. The result of this purchase was that the group home did not lose power during the storm, which allowed them to stay in the house and not evacuate as so many others around them had to do.

Business Outreach Center Capital Network is a microenterprise/small business development organization that provides customized business services and loans to underserved entrepreneurs in New York City and Newark, New Jersey.

What new relief efforts or programs is your CDFI contemplating if any to help in the aftermath of Superstorm Sandy?

Responses: 11

All respondents are planning some sort of aid to the victims of Superstorm Sandy. While each plan provides unique features, CCG Community Partners succinctly describes CDFI efforts in its Superstorm Sandy Implementation Plan that applies in general to all respondents:

1. Communicate with all existing stakeholders, community residents, governmental leaders, developers, sponsors, and local organizations to assess status and need;

2. Identify high-impact cornerstone and infrastructure projects with a priority focus on community job creation and restoration or replacement of core services such as food, medicine, shelter, and education;

3. Enhance existing investment strategies and develop new approaches for the storm-affected regions;

4. Underwrite and realistically prioritize these potential investments to achieve the greatest community impact over a sustainable platform that will encourage long-term revitalization;

5. Serve as a communications nexus point to connect equity and debt sources with potential investment opportunities within areas devastated by Superstorm Sandy;

6. Coordinate specific equity and debt investors to help finance future CDFI Fund investments;[6] and

7. Aggressively promote new discussions with non-traditional leveraged lenders.

Specific initiatives by CDFIs include low-cost, emergency business loans of up to $10,000 to businesses in all five boroughs of New York City by the Business Outreach Center Capital. The loans are interest-free for six months and 3 percent thereafter when a client signs up for Automated Clearing House (ACH) payments.

Community Development Corporation of Long Island is determining what kind of specialized loan products, if any, they should introduce to small businesses and homeowners recovering from the storm. They also plan to be a referral source for other available funding for relief efforts.

Enterprise Community Partners created the Enterprise Partner Support & Rebuilding Fund to help its partners with immediate recovery and rebuilding efforts (see page 20 for more detail). As of November 14, 2012, Enterprise has provided eight grants to partners totaling $145,000, supporting approximately 475 affordable housing units:

- Tri-City Peoples, East Orange, New Jersey: Grant to fund Tri-City's facilities crew to work with individual homeowners on yard cleanup and debris removal, including renting a dumpster. The beneficiaries are primarily senior, fixed-income homeowners.

- Carroll Gardens Association: Grant toward boiler replacement on two projects and for projected income loss during the aftermath of Superstorm Sandy.

- Lower East Side Peoples Mutual Housing Corporation: Grant toward elevator parts, boiler replacements, professional bills, and employee overtime for several buildings.

- Metropolitan Council on Jewish Poverty: Grant toward architectural and engineering costs of assessment and rehabilitation work on Abraham 1, a project that had to be evacuated.

- Lower East Side Center: Grant to support all relief efforts, such as bringing in a temporary boiler, purchasing items for client's warmth and safety and securing funds for staffing time. The funds will also assist in efforts to fix the elevator.

- Asian Americans for Equality: Grant to maintain intake, outreach, and counseling staff in their Sandy Emergency Help Center (Center) located in Flushing. The Center is a collaboration with Assembly-elect Ron Kim and One Flushing Economic Development Center, to assist small immigrant business owners affected by Hurricane Sandy with FEMA registration, loan application, and other assistance.

---

[6] CCG Community Partners used this method of finance in response to Hurricane Katrina and the BP Oil Disaster, and reports that its core institutional partners have always shown significant support for the CCG Community Partners mission. Together, Bank of America, PNC Bank, US Bank, and Wells Fargo Bank have invested more than $363 million of both equity and debt with CCG Community Partners and its controlling entity, including more than $163 million of NMTC equity.

St. John's Bread & Life
Brooklyn & Queens, New York
CDFI: Low Income Investment Fund

The Low Income Investment Fund (LIIF) provides a wide range of products and services in low-income communities including the support of non-profit service providers that serve extremely poor and vulnerable communities, such as soup kitchens. Many of these organizations were in the process of planning for the additional needs during the holiday season before Superstorm Sandy. After the storm, these groups were inundated with requests for food, clothes, supplies, and services. One such group, St. John's Bread & Life, a previous NMTC allocation recipient from LIIF, serves meals, operates a food

pantry, and provides health and social services in Brooklyn and Queens. One of St. John's ongoing programs is a mobile soup kitchen that extends its reach to other areas of the city. With demand for food running high in the days after Superstorm Sandy, St. John's sent out its mobile soup kitchen and began serving thousands of meals in and around Coney Island. In addition, St. John's delivered thousands of blankets to people in housing developments who lost heat and to displaced people who sought refuge in condemned buildings without power or gas. LIIF is providing funding to St. John's to support its quick and critical relief efforts.

- Surf Gardens New York Foundation for Senior Citizens: Grant will be used to replace a portion of HUD Section 8 subsidy revenue that was lost for the month of November and help to ensure that the building's operating costs including employee salaries and benefits, 24-hour security service, utilities, administrative, maintenance, and other operating expenses are met.

- Community Agency for Senior Citizens: Grant to support properties physical rehabilitation work due to damage from Superstorm Sandy.

As a real estate lender for affordable housing and community facilities, Leviticus 25:23 Alternative Fund, Inc. knows that housing reconstruction will be the paramount need, specifically in Staten Island, Queens, Brooklyn, and the south shore of Long Island. Leviticus 25:23 Alternative Fund, Inc. plans to help with financing for the repair of damage caused by Hurricane Sandy to low-income housing and community facilities serving low-income communities, as well as financing to non-profit service providers for the repair of damage to their properties or for the purchase or construction of new space to expand services.

The Low Income Investment Fund has committed $1 million to support immediate relief efforts (see page 21 for details). LIIF is providing low-cost loans and grants to organizations that are responding to and/or were damaged by the storm. Housing the people who were displaced by the storm has been identified as one of the key challenges of the post-Sandy rebuilding efforts. Therefore, LIIF is participating in a multifamily lender working group convened by the New York City Department of Housing Preservation and Development to create financing that meets the longer-term needs of privately-owned multifamily housing in New York City.

The Nonprofit Finance Fund continues to seek opportunities to lend to clients that are applying to FEMA and/or support from the Small Business Administration, or are submitting insurance claims.

Leviticus 25:23 Alternative Fund, Inc. provided funding for a 12-unit affordable housing project in Westchester County. Luckily, the housing was not affected by Superstorm Sandy, but the CDFI is presently assessing how its particular type of flexible capital can be put to use by those affected by the storm. As a real estate lender for affordable housing and community facilities, Leviticus 25:23 Alternative Fund, Inc. expects that its usefulness will be in the reconstruction effort rather than immediate relief.

New Jersey Community Capital has been contacted by several of its investors as well as local communities and the State of New Jersey to provide disaster relief to businesses negatively impacted by Hurricane Sandy. New Jersey Community Capital has established the Rebuild New Jersey Fund, which will provided interim financing in amounts between $10,000 and $30,000 for small businesses impacted by the storm.

The Primary Care Development Corporation supports efforts to provide CDFIs that serve communities impacted by Sandy with additional resources to assist in recovery efforts. While the CDFI has not planned any special lending programs, it is offering bridge and mini-perm loans to borrowers.

Historically, Seedco Financial Services has played a major role in the post-disaster economic recovery efforts that were implemented in the wake of the 9/11 terrorist attacks, Hurricanes Katrina, Rita, and Gustav, the Gulf Coast BP Oil Spill, and other disruptions from power outages and manmade disasters. SFS is developing the initial phase of a Small Business Recovery Initiative that will be geared to address a targeted set of disaster recovery-related needs for small businesses that suffered from storm-related damage. SFS's immediate goal is to target a highly-impacted location in New York City and focus upon addressing the needs of one or more of the community's critical small business sectors. For example, SFS is contemplating developing a targeted set of financial and technical assistance services specifically for contractors (electrical, plumbing, etc.) in Staten Island with the intent to enable them to quickly restore their operating capacity and actively start participating in the long-term rebuilding process.

The Disability Opportunity Fund is planning for new clients: people with disabilities and the organizations which serve them on Long Island in the New York/New Jersey area affected by Superstorm Sandy that will need financing, as well as technical assistance. The CDFI is coordinating its efforts with organizations such as Long Island Housing Partnership, Catholic Charities, and the Episcopal Church to locate usable housing stock.

Special Funds Established by CDFIs

"As a CDFI, we understand that after the 'first responders' leave the area, funds will be needed to rebuild our communities. The DOF is preparing to do its part by dedicating a portion of our portfolio to respond to 'Sandy-related' financing requests."

Charles D. Hammerman, President & CEO, The Disability Opportunity Fund

Accion
Sandy Recovery Business Loan Program

Accion East and Online, a leading U.S. microlender with over 20 years of lending history in New York City, has created a special fund, the Sandy Recovery Business Loan Program, which is targeted to small business owners who will not qualify under traditional loans or existing emergency loan programs due to low credit scores, limited financial records, and/or the need for greater monthly payment flexibility. The program offers loans up to $25,000, with zero interest and no payments for the first three months and a fixed 4.99 percent rate thereafter. In addition, each small business owner under the program will receive a grant equal to 15 percent of the loan amount to accelerate their recovery efforts.

"Our program is aimed at serving the most credit-challenged and informal sector of the New York economy, "said Paul Quintero, CEO of Accion East and Online. "This program exists because many caring individuals and institutions realized that quickly supporting vulnerable and small business owners was critical to the economic landscape of New York City."

Initial supporters for the program included thousands of individuals through Groupon's online and grassroots fundraising platform, The Robin Hood Foundation and a local philanthropist created the initial $250,000 loan fund in early November. Soon thereafter, Accion received support from Morgan Stanley, Bank of America Merchant Services, and Union Bank to increase the loan fund to $500,000. The JPMorgan Chase Foundation provided a $250,000 grant to expand the loan fund to $725,000. This funding enables Accion to provide $108,000 in direct grants, creating a unique feature for the program and an extra boost for entrepreneurial success.

"In order for small businesses to rebuild and recover from Hurricane Sandy, access to capital is critical," said Audrey Choi, Managing Director and Head of Global Sustainable Finance at Morgan Stanley. "Accion's program will help rebuild businesses while also promoting longer-term sustainable economic development in the communities where they operate."

To date, Accion has closed 15 loans totaling $200,000 under the program and has over $600,000 in additional demand. Accion's process is fast, with a historical turnaround time of less than 10 days from application to disbursement.

Enterprise Partner Support and Rebuilding Fund

Enterprise is strongly committed to recovery, rebuilding, and resilience. Enterprise has worked closely with its partners over the past seven years to rebuild nearly 10,000 homes along the Gulf Coast following Hurricane Katrina, and they have learned that transparency, coordination, and patience are critical to recovering from an event of this magnitude.

Enterprise had launched the Partner Support and Rebuilding Fund (Fund) to provide financial assistance to help its affordable housing partners with immediate recovery and rebuilding efforts. The Fund consists of two components: emergency grants to be used to address any immediate needs resulting from the storm, including purchasing of supplies, equipment, deposits, fees needed to hire contractors, and/or other resources to support displaced families; and low-cost working capital for affordable housing development partners to use to speed rebuilding, including bridging the gap to other resources (both public and private) and insurance coverage.

Enterprise has helped to create more than 35,000 affordable homes throughout the New York, New Jersey, and Connecticut region. They are working directly with affordable housing owners and managers to assess storm damage, identify resources available for repair, and fill capacity gaps to ensure that building systems are brought back online quickly. In doing so, Enterprise is leveraging its partners' capacity with the organization's expertise in asset management, construction management, and energy services. This combined effort is designed to ensure that there is appropriate attention given to both the pace and quality of repairs.

Enterprise's experience in Gulf recovery efforts has raised the need for quality data analysis to assess the long- and short-term impacts of recovery efforts. Enterprise's Knowledge Impact and Strategy (KIS) team has produced helpful analytical tools, maps, and graphs that use public data to identify affected areas. Enterprise is working with local academic partners to broaden this effort to create a "recovery index," which would track the recovery process, population, investment, and other key indicators.

The City of New York's Department of Housing Preservation and Development department has convened Enterprise and other local intermediaries to develop a programmatic and financial response to the significant loss of and damage to one- to four-unit family homes. Additionally, in coordination with local agencies, Enterprise is identifying vacant apartments within its housing portfolio to temporarily house families displaced by storm damage. They are also working with community partners to make new apartments that are just completing construction available for displaced families. At least 100 apartments have been identified to date.

"The devastation unleashed by the storm reminds us all of the importance of having a safe place to call home, and of helping neighbors in need. It will take a coordinated effort among the public and private sectors and philanthropy to rebuild effectively. It will take years for the communities devastated by Superstorm Sandy to fully recover, but together we will rebuild stronger than ever."

Terri Ludwig, President & CEO, Enterprise Community Partners

Low Income Investment Fund $1 Million to Communities Affected by Sandy

To support recovery efforts, the Low Income Investment Fund has committed $1 million to ensure that those hardest hit by the storm have access to food and much needed services.

LIIF's New York staff has reached out to its local network to understand the needs in the communities they serve. As a result, LIIF is providing deeply subsidized loans and grants to grocery stores and social service non-profit clients that operate in areas of high need, such as the Rockaways, Coney Island, and Staten Island. These organizations can use the funds for inventory, facilities repair, and working capital so they can re-establish themselves in their local communities.

Among the first projects that LIIF has supported is St. John's Bread & Life, an emergency food provider that has been using its mobile soup kitchen in the immediate aftermath of the storm to deliver thousands of meals and supplies to affected areas. Already in the process of gearing up for the holidays, Bread & Life has added emergency outreach efforts to families who continue to grapple with displacement, ongoing power outages, and hunger.

LIIF is also committed to rebuilding neighborhoods and helping families and businesses return to their communities. LIIF is providing funds to rebuild a Key Food store in Coney Island operated by Amy and Joe Doleh. The husband and wife entrepreneurs opened the store in 2009 and previously received financing from LIIF to break ground on a new Key Food in Staten Island. Located in one of the most affected areas of New York, the Dolehs' Coney Island store was flooded with five feet of water. After the storm, the store was unfortunately further damaged by looters. The Dolehs will use the funding from LIIF to repair the building and restock their shelves, so they can get back to providing groceries to their neighbors.

LIIF is fully committed to continuing to find ways to support vulnerable families, help small businesses get back on their feet, and rebuild communities affected by this disaster.

The Low Income Investment Fund has invested in the poorest communities in the New York and Mid-Atlantic region for over two decades. We are deeply committed to responding to people's immediate needs and to the long-term rebuilding of communities affected by the storm."

Nancy O. Andrews, President & CEO, Low Income Investment Fund

Survey Respondents

Accion is a leader in U.S. microfinance and is committed to bringing affordable small business loans to microentrepreneurs. Accion has provided over $132 million in over 20,000 microloans since inception in 1991, helping to grow small businesses and strengthen the communities they serve. Its lending model is the product of 45 years of Accion experience in providing credit to low- to moderate-income individuals worldwide, customized to meet the unique needs of small businesses operating in the United States. Accion's lending philosophy is focused on credit building, financial education, and community partnerships.

CDFI Fund Award History for Accion USA & New York		
Award Type	**Year**	**Award Amount**
CORE	1998	$800,000
CORE	1998	$500,000
CORE	2000	$1,500,000
CORE	2001	$53,000
CORE	2001	$1,750,000
FA	2004	$584,850
TA	2004	$50,000
FA	2008	$1,000,000
FA	2010	$750,000

Business Outreach Center Capital Network's (BOC) mission is to improve the economic prospects of traditionally underserved groups, with a focus on low- and moderate-income entrepreneurs and their communities. BOC is a microenterprise/small business development organization with over a decade-long record of delivering customized business services to underserved entrepreneurs in New York City and Newark, New Jersey, as well as capacity-building services to organizations establishing and operating community and microenterprise development programs.

CDFI Fund Award History for Business Outreach Center Capital Network		
Award Type	**Year**	**Award Amount**
SECA	2002	$102,000
FA	2006	$300,000
FA	2009	$600,000
TA	2010	$100,000
FA	2011	$600,000

Moussa Ba: Street vendor
Lower Manhattan, New York
CDFI: Business Outreach Center Capital

Moussa Ba is a street vendor in lower Manhattan and a long time BOC Capital loan client. Mr. Ba kept his inventory and vendor equipment in a storage facility that was completely flooded in Lower Manhattan. He is claiming a total loss of his business and has been approved and provided with an $8,000 BOC Capital Disaster Recovery loan to start back up again. To help with his current loan BOC Capital rolled his outstanding loan balance into the new recovery loan that has a lower interest rate and payment deferments built in to help with cash flow as he begins to recover his business.

CCG Community Partners, LLC is a New Jersey-based CDE. Utilizing New Markets Tax Credits, CCG Community Partners, LLC, an affiliate of CityScape Capital Group, offers investment capital to owners of commercial properties located within qualified low-income communities. The majority of CCG Community Partners' activities (98 percent) is targeted to providing equity in and/or loans to Qualified Low-Income Community Businesses for purposes of developing and rehabilitating commercial real estate.

CDFI Fund Award History for CCG Community Partners, LLC		
Award Type	**Year**	**Award Amount**
NMTC	2005	$50,000,000
NMTC	2006	$43,000,000
NMTC	2007	$40,000,000
NMTC	2008	$20,000,000
NMTC	2010	$42,000,000
NMTC	2011	$25,000,000

Community Development Corporation of Long Island (CDC of Long Island) is committed to making dreams of long-term economic stability come true. Supporting clients through innovative programs and services is the most valuable service CDC of Long Island can provide. In 1969, a group of concerned Long Islanders came together to address the growing demand for non-discriminatory affordable housing opportunities. CDC of Long Island now employs over 90 people, serves both Nassau and Suffolk counties, and provides a variety of programs and services that address the dynamic challenges faced by those who live and work on Long Island. CDC supports the housing and economic aspirations of individuals, families, and small businesses through exemplary stewardship of resources entrusted to the CDFI.

CDFI Fund Award History for Community Development Corporation of Long Island		
Award Type	**Year**	**Award Amount**
SECA	1999	$27,500
CORE	2000	$600,000
CORE	2001	$800,000
FA	2004	$782,500

Enterprise Community Loan Fund is a national CDFI working in all 50 U.S. states to provide affordable and flexible capital to help create dynamic communities where families have access to quality housing, transit, key services, and community facilities. For 30 years, Enterprise has introduced solutions through public-private partnerships with financial institutions, governments, community organizations, and other partners that share its vision that one day, every person will have an affordable home in a vibrant community, filled with promise and the opportunity for a good life.

CDFI Fund Award History for Enterprise Community Loan Fund & Subsidiaries		
Award Type	**Year**	**Award Amount**
CORE	1997	$2,500,000
CORE	1998	$2,500,000
NMTC	2002	$25,000,000
NMTC	2002	$90,000,000
NMTC	2003	$140,000,000
NMTC	2003	$55,000,000
FA	2005	$1,398,750
NMTC	2005	$80,000,000
NMTC	2006	$105,000,000
FA	2007	$860,000
NMTC	2007	$12,000,000
NMTC	2007	$100,000,000
NMTC	2008	$95,000,000
FA	2008	$1,000,000
NMTC	2008	$20,000,000
NMTC	2009	$10,000,000
FA	2010	$750,000
NMTC	2010	$62,000,000
FA	2011	$1,500,000
FA	2012	$1,453,806

"We will apply our experience working with partners to rebuild the Gulf Coast in the wake of Hurricane Katrina to similar efforts along the East Coast."

Terri Ludwig, President & CEO, Enterprise Community Partners

Empire State Development Corporation (ESD) is New York's chief economic development agency. The mission of Empire State Development is to promote a vigorous and growing economy, encourage the creation of new job and economic opportunities, increase revenues to the State and its municipalities, and achieve stable and diversified local economies. Through the use of loans, grants, tax credits, and other forms of financial assistance, Empire State Development strives to enhance private business investment and growth to spur job creation and support prosperous communities across New York State.

The **Leviticus 25:23 Alternative Fund, Inc.** is a non-profit financial intermediary, motivated by faith, which offers investors a socially-responsive means to serve low-income neighborhoods. The Leviticus 25:23 Alternative Fund provides flexible capital and financial services for the development of affordable housing and community facilities, especially child care centers, throughout New York, New Jersey, and Connecticut.

CDFI Fund Award History for Leviticus 25:23 Alternative Fund, Inc.		
Award Type	**Year**	**Award Amount**
CORE	1997	$250,000
CORE	2001	$550,000
TA	2004	$47,032
FA	2005	$902,500
TA	2007	$66,430
FA	2009	$2,000,000
FA	2012	$1,262,179

The Low Income Investment Fund (LIIF) invests capital to support healthy families and communities. Since 1984, LIIF has served one million people by investing $1 billion in a range of strategies from housing to education to environmentally sustainable projects. Over its history, LIIF has supported efforts to create and preserve: 56,000 units of affordable housing; 180,000 child care spaces; 56,000 spaces in schools; and 3.5 million square feet of community facilities and commercial space. LIIF's work has generated $21 billion in family income and societal benefits. LIIF has offices in San Francisco, Los Angeles, New York City and Washington, D.C.

CDFI Fund Award History for Low Income Investment Fund		
Award Type	**Year**	**Award Amount**
CORE	1996	$2,500,000
CORE	1997	$165,000
CORE	1998	$2,000,000
SECA	1999	$50,000
CORE	2000	$1,000,000
CORE	2001	$1,950,000
FA	2003	$1,320,000
FA	2006	$585,000
FA	2007	$860,000
NMTC	2007	$44,000,000
FA	2008	$1,000,000
NMTC	2008	$50,000,000
FA	2009	$2,000,000
NMTC	2009	$45,000,000
CMF	2010	$6,000,000
FA	2010	$750,000
NMTC	2010	$21,000,000
FA	2011	$1,500,000
HFFI-FA	2011	$3,000,000
NMTC	2011	$50,000,000

Nonprofit Finance Fund® (NFF), a certified CDFI, makes millions of dollars in loans to non-profits and pushes for fundamental improvement in how money is given and used in the sector. Since 1980, NFF has worked to connect money to mission effectively so that non-profits can keep doing what they do so well. NFF has lent over $235 million and leveraged $1.3 billion of capital investment on behalf of its clients. In partnership with others, NFF has generated $16 million for non-profits for building reserves, cash reserves, and endowments. NFF has also provided $1.2 million in loan guarantees, $10.3 million in 9/11 recovery grants, about $13 million in capital grants, and $2 million in planning grants.

CDFI Fund Award History for Nonprofit Finance Fund®		
Award Type	**Year**	**Award Amount**
CORE	1996	$1,000,000
CORE	1998	$1,000,000
CORE	1999	$1,900,000
CORE	2001	$1,000,000
FA	2006	$585,000
NMTC	2006	$20,000,000
NMTC	2008	$50,000,000
FA	2009	$1,900,000
NMTC	2009	$60,000,000
FA	2010	$750,000
NMTC	2010	$21,000,000
FA	2011	$1,500,000
NMTC	2011	$40,000,000
FA	2012	$1,453,806
HFFI-FA	2012	$750,000

New Jersey Community Capital is a non-profit CDFI that provides innovative financing and technical assistance to organizations that support housing and sustainable community development ventures that increase jobs, improve education, and strengthen neighborhoods. New Jersey Community Capital offers loan capital that is broader than bank lending to results-oriented, socially responsible organizations that are committed to creating positive change in low- to moderate-income communities throughout New Jersey. New Jersey Community Capital effectively combines expertise with innovation and dedication to deliver high-impact community development solutions that change lives for the better.

CDFI Fund Award History for New Jersey Community Capital		
Award Type	**Year**	**Award Amount**
CORE	1997	$1,230,000
CORE	2000	$3,030,000
NMTC	2002	$15,000,000
FA	2004	$1,000,000
FA	2008	$1,000,000
NMTC	2008	$35,000,000
FA	2009	$2,000,000
FA	2010	$750,000
FA	2011	$1,500,000
FA	2012	$1,453,806

"Immediate needs include temporary housing for those displaced; short-term funding for businesses that sustained some damage but are able to open and operate relatively quickly; and assistance to put some 'normalcy' back into people's lives."

Wayne T. Meyer, President, New Jersey Community Capital

Primary Care Development Corporation (PCDC) is a non-profit organization dedicated to expanding and transforming primary care in underserved communities to improve health outcomes, lower health costs, and reduce disparities. PCDC provides the capital and know-how to build, renovate, and expand community-based health facilities, so that providers can deliver the best care to their patients. PCDC also provides consulting, training, and coaching services to help practices deliver a patient-centered model of care that maximizes patient access, meaningful use of health IT, care coordination, and patient experience. The PCDC business model maintains a mission-driven approach that values measurable impact, system change, and sustainability.

CDFI Fund Award History for Primary Care Development Corporation		
Award Type	**Year**	**Award Amount**
CORE	1997	$2,500,000
SECA	1999	$41,000
FA	2003	$2,000,000
NMTC	2007	$40,000,000
FA	2008	$1,000,000
FA	2009	$2,000,000
FA	2010	$750,000
FA	2011	$1,500,000

"Primary Care Development Corporation clients that were directly impacted were closed for a minimum of two and as many as 10 days, due primarily to loss of power. These clients estimate the associated loss of revenues to range from $200,000 up to $2,000,000 (as much as 4 percent of annual revenues). As city, state, and federal agencies determine how we can better prepare for future disasters, PCDC will continue to work for stronger primary care involvement and resources in overall planning and response efforts."

Ronda Kotelchuck, CEO, Primary Care Development Corporation

Seedco Financial Services, Inc. (SFS) is a national non-profit organization with more than $70 million in assets under management. SFS seeks to stimulate economic development in communities that are underserved by traditional banking institutions by providing affordable capital, hands-on business assistance, and innovative solutions to small businesses, non-profit organizations, and real estate developers. SFS's lending activities are designed to strengthen the capacity of faith-based and community organizations, community development corporations, small businesses, and large-scale development projects. Headquartered in New York, SFS also maintains offices in Alabama and Louisiana.

CDFI Fund Award History for Seedco Financial Services, Inc.		
Award Type	**Year**	**Award Amount**
FA	2007	$407,000
FA	2009	$2,000,000
FA	2010	$750,000
FA	2011	$1,500,000
FA	2012	$1,453,806

The **Disability Opportunity Fund** (DOF) is a CDFI that was launched in April 2007. DOF is located in Albertson, New York and operates nationally. DOF is a non-profit organization dedicated to providing housing opportunities for and advancing the needs of people with disabilities and their families.

CDFI Fund Award History for The Disability Opportunity Fund		
Award Type	**Year**	**Award Amount**
TA	2009	$87,519
FA	2012	$600,000

Appendix 1: CDFI Fund Letter

November 14, 2012

Dear Friends,

First and foremost, our hearts go out to those affected by the destruction of Superstorm Sandy. As we all know, CDFIs, day in and day out, are on the front lines providing vital financing and services to underserved communities across our country. CDFIs have and will play an extremely important role in supporting the recovery in those communities on the East Coast that are in dire need at this time.

I realize that you have probably not yet absorbed the impact on your organization and the customers you serve, but I ask that you take a few moments to help us understand what you are facing now and going forward. Please send your response no later than November 30th to PublicAffairsOffice@cdfi.treas.gov.

Your CDFI

- Was your CDFI impacted by Superstorm Sandy? If so, how?
- Did you sustain damage (i.e. electricity out; water damage, etc.)?
- Have you reopened for business, and if so when?
- What are your needs moving forward?
- Are you currently involved in or providing any direct recovery assistance services?

Your Clients/Customers

- Have any of your clients/customers been impacted? If so, could you provide an example or two of these projects/investments (small business, housing, etc.) and provide a short narrative as to what happened, what was your investment, and what are the needs moving forward?

The Future

- What new relief efforts or programs is your CDFI contemplating if any to help in the aftermath of Superstorm Sandy?

Please Spread The Word

Survivors of this storm can take the first steps toward recovery right now by registering for assistance with FEMA. Impacted residents and business owners in New Jersey, New York, Connecticut and West Virginia can apply for federal assistance by phone 1-800-621-FEMA (3362), via mobile devices at m.fema.gov or online at www.DisasterAssistance.gov.

Please know that you are in our thoughts at this time of great need.

Sincerely,

Donna J. Gambrell, Director

CDFI Response to Superstorm Sandy

Appendix 2: CDFI/CDE Investment in the path of Superstorm Sandy

CONNECTICUT

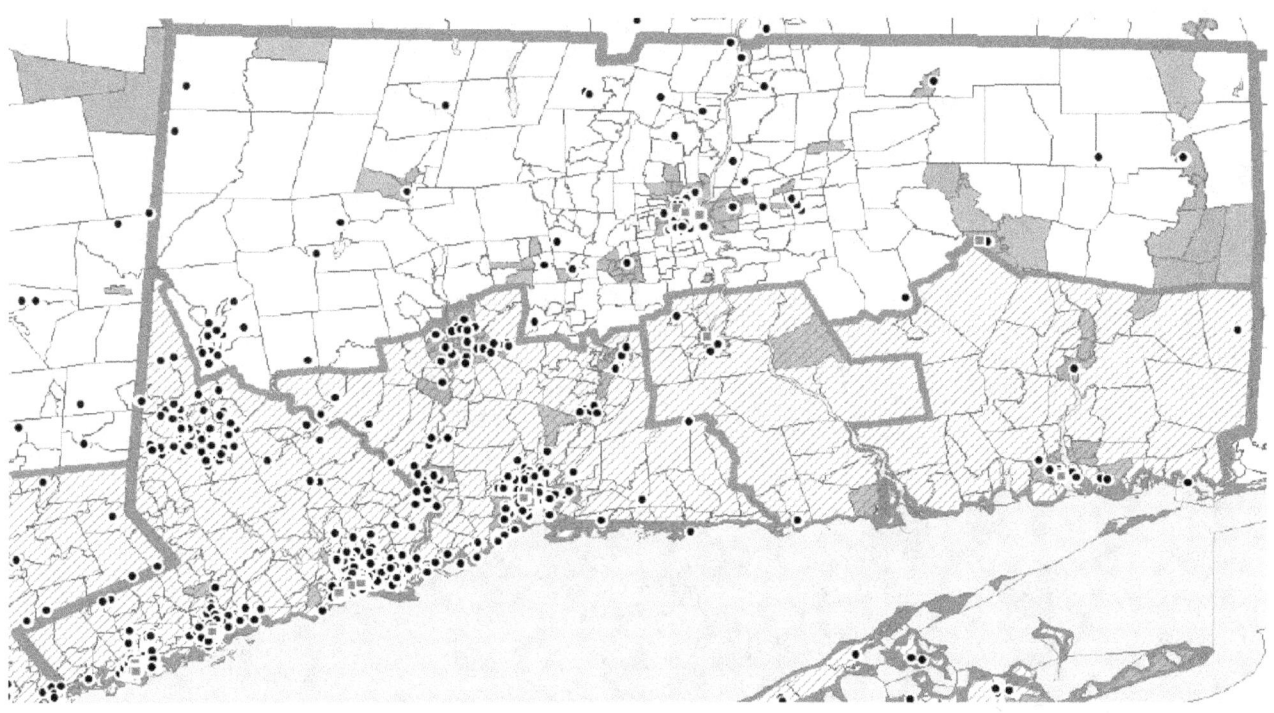

Census Tracts by Eligibility

☐	Not Eligible
▨	Both CDFI and NMTC Eligible
▨	CDFI Only
●	CDFI Loan/Investment
▣	NMTC Project
▨	Hurricane Sandy FEMA Disaster Areas

Created by the CDFI Fund, U.S. Department of the Treasury, December 18, 2012.
Sources: CDFI Fund's Community Investment Impact System (CIIS), 2003-2012;
U.S. Census Bureau 2000 Census; Bureau of Labor Statistics.

Location of CDFI Loans and Investments and
NMTC Projects Relative to Eligible Census Tracts

NEW JERSEY

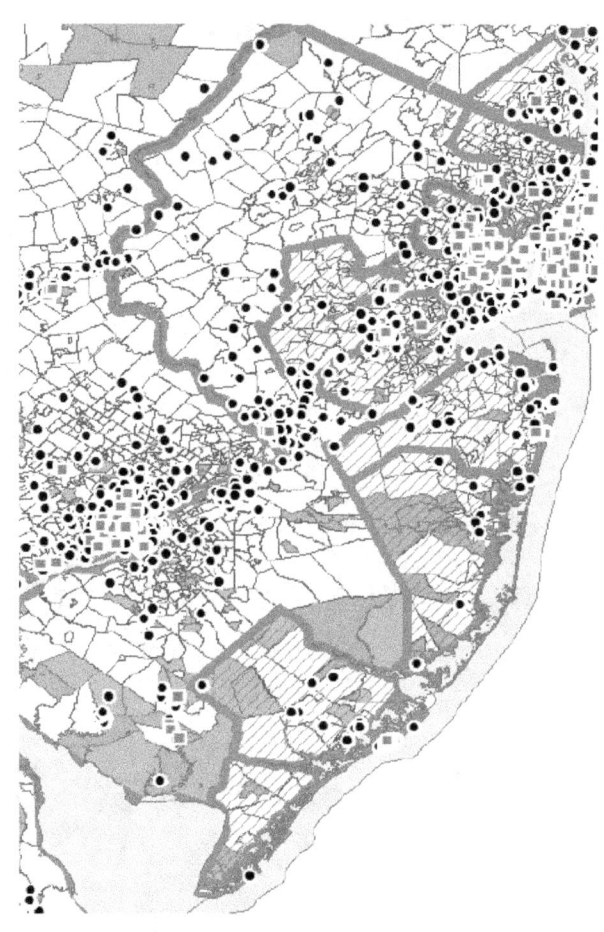

Census Tracts by Eligibility

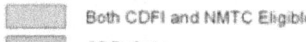

Not Eligible

Both CDFI and NMTC Eligible

CDFI Only

● CDFI Loan/Investment

■ NMTC Project

▨ Hurricane Sandy FEMA Disaster Areas

Created by the CDFI Fund, U.S. Department of the Treasury, December 18, 2012.
Sources: CDFI Fund's Community Investment Impact System (CIIS), 2003-2012;
U.S. Census Bureau 2000 Census; Bureau of Labor Statistics.

Location of CDFI Loans and Investments and NMTC Projects Relative to Eligible Census Tracts

NEW YORK AND LONG ISLAND

Census Tracts by Eligibility

	Not Eligible
	Both CDFI and NMTC Eligible
	CDFI Only
●	CDFI Loan/Investment
■	NMTC Project
⧄	Hurricane Sandy FEMA Disaster Areas

Created by the CDFI Fund, U.S. Department of the Treasury, December 18, 2012.
Sources: CDFI Fund's Community Investment Impact System (CIIS), 2003-2012;
U.S. Census Bureau 2000 Census; Bureau of Labor Statistics.

Location of CDFI Loans and Investments and
NMTC Projects Relative to Eligible Census Tracts

Appendix 3: Abbreviations & Acronyms

CDFI Fund: Community Development Financial Institutions Fund

CDFI: Community Development Financial Institutions

CMF: Capital Magnet Fund

CORE: CDFI Program Financial Assistance Award

FA: CDFI Program Financial Assistance Award

HFFI-FA: Healthy Foods Financing Initiative-Financial Assistance

HFFI-TA: Healthy Foods Financing Initiative-Technical Assistance

NMTC: New Markets Tax Credits

SECA: CDFI Program Small and/or Emerging CDFI Financial Assistance Award